TIME AND WORKLOAD MANAGEMENT

TIME AND WORKLOAD MANAGEMENT

Debra Allcock

The Industrial Society

First published in 1995 by
The Industrial Society
Robert Hyde House
48 Bryanston Square
London W1H 7LN
Telephone: 0171-262 2401

© *The Industrial Society 1995*
Reprinted 1997
ISBN 1 85835 154 5

British Library Cataloguing-in-Publication Data.
A Catalogue record for this book is available from the
British Library.

Typeset by: The Midlands Book Typesetting Company
Printed by: Lavenham Press
Cover Design: Pylon

The Industrial Society is a Registered
Charity No. 290003

Contents

Introduction

A recent survey on how managers use their time at work shows that 20.4% of a manager's working week is wasted. This works out at an average of 1 in 5 working days. Interruptions by phone or people dropping in are the two quoted major instances of time wasted at work. Poor lateral communication is another 'time criminal'. The survey showed that 90.3% of directors and managers work with a cluttered desk, 33% of management time is spent dealing with routine paperwork and wasted time at work results in a cost of 20% of management time. 12% of the working week is spent travelling.

Time is always quoted as being an important resource. However, we tend to view time wasted as the fault of others rather than ourselves. We need better equipment, people should communicate better with us, people should not interrupt us and so on. Lack of time is often used as a cover for inefficient working methods, lack of planning or forethought, delays and failures to meet agreed deadlines.

The reality is that we do not live in an ideal world and we therefore have to achieve good results in the time available with the resources that we have.

Proper management of time is crucial to the success of an organisation, yet so much is left to chance. Time management and work management are essentially down to self discipline. The system that we choose to help to make better use of our time is, in a sense, irrelevant. Any system is only as good as the person who operates it. There are no magic wands which will suddenly make us good at managing our time. There is only deciding what our priorities are and concentrating on them.

It's worth remembering the following:

- There are **8760** hours available in the year
- **2920** spent sleeping
- **1928** spent at work
- **1664** hours available at weekends (not including sleeping)
- **320** hours of holiday (not including weekends) depending on our holiday allowance
- **1446** hours 'spare' during the working week (bearing in mind that actually it's really half of this i.e., 723, if you use the example above as a guideline)
- **482** hours travelling

Given that we cannot *make* more time, we need to make the most of the hours we spend at work and those we have available to spend on ourselves. This book aims to give some ideas how to maximise the usage of our available hours, to balance the time spent at home and the time spent at work and to use all the hours that are available to fulfil needs and priorities.

The Psychology of Time

We all have a lot of things to fit into our lives. We need to achieve our objectives at work and our objectives at home as well. Yet we know there isn't a huge amount of time available.

We are all aware that we waste time, but can often not be specific about exactly how much time we waste.

A recent survey showed the **Top Time Wasters** at work to be (ranked in order):

1. Telephone interruptions
2. People dropping by
3. Poor information exchange between departments
4. Problems with computers – 'technofailure'
5. Change in priorities caused by colleagues

6. Lack of organisational planning
7. Poor listening skills of others
8. Inappropriate organisation structure
9. Moving goal posts
10. Putting things right that were not right first time
11. Indecision
12. Badly organised and chaired meetings
13. Distractions in the place of work
14. Over bureaucratic office procedures
15. Unnecessary checking on others' work and your own work

'Checking for understanding' is also quoted as a time waster. People, in particular managers, often assume that because no questions were asked the people they have spoken to have understood exactly what was said.

Some time we see as 'expendable' and some not. For example, many of us think nothing of working late or bringing work home, yet we are actually stealing time from our families. What would you prefer on your epitaph: *"S/he worked long and hard hours"* or, *"S/he spent a lot of time with his/her family and friends"*? *"S/he was appreciated by her managers"* or, *"S/he was loved by her family"*? When planning what you are going to spend your time on, you really need to think not just about work priorities but also about your life priorities.

We tend not to see time as a truly valuable commodity. Although, we often hear people say that *'time is money'*, many of us don't behave as if it is as important as money. If someone stole our wallet with £50 in it, the chances are we would give chase and try to recover your money. If someone stole 50 minutes of our time, we would probably just let it go. This is mainly because our perception is that money is tangible and time isn't. If we were told we had won £1 million we would probably go off and buy all sorts of luxury items that we don't really need, simply because we are now in possession of an extra £1 million. However, if we were given £1 million and told that that was **all** the money we would **ever** have for the rest of our life, we would be much more likely to make very careful decisions about how we invested it and what we spent it on.

Life is a bit like having £1 million with no more to come. We have on average 72 years available. In this life at least, there is no more. Yet we probably take time very much for granted, spending it willy nilly and not really counting the cost.

Work out for yourself how much time you are wasting doing things that, if you thought about it properly, you probably wouldn't do at all.

Before you can start to plan on what and when you spend your time, you need to be sure exactly how much you have available and what you have to spend it on. Managing and budgeting time is very similar to how you manage and budget your money. You know exactly how much money you will be given at the end of each month in your salary. You also know exactly how much you need to set aside for your mortgage/rent, the bills, food etc. You therefore know how much is left over which you can afford to spend on luxury items like a new frock, a new suit or a holiday. If in any given month you receive a particularly large bill you adjust your money accordingly and don't buy the new frock, but pay the telephone bill instead.

You need to identify for yourself how much of your time needs to be spent on the time equivalent of a mortgage (the 'time mortgage') and what you can spend on the "time new frock" i.e., something that you don't need to do.

We are quite good at budgeting time to carry out specific tasks in our personal lives, but forget all those basic good principles as soon as we get into work. For example, if you are going on holiday and need to catch an aeroplane, you will often allow yourself extra time to get to the airport in case something goes wrong. Similarly, if you are holding a dinner party, you will mentally calculate what time you need to put the food in the oven, what time you need to go and get ready (for example, you shower and change while the potatoes are cooking) and how long each different item of food takes so that you can have it all hot on the table at the same time. You lay the table earlier in the day and delegate tasks to the rest of the family or friends. Unfortunately, most of us are probably not as organised as this at work. Things often go wrong at work because unlike choosing how to spend our salary money, we are not as careful or as conscious about how we choose to spend our time salary.

Time spent doing things we enjoy seems to move quickly and time spent doing things we hate seems to move slowly. Obviously, all the time is moving at the same rate and it is simply our perception of it that has changed. Waiting for a train seems to take ages, (particularly if it's raining!), yet the time spent on holiday seems to go very quickly.

There are also times when we allow other people to dictate to us what we do. We allow other people's choice of when they telephone us to dictate what we spend that time doing (i.e. replying to their telephone call). We allow the post room in our organisations to dictate what time we open the post (i.e. when it arrives). We allow British Rail to dictate what time and how long we take travelling to work, and so on. Although some of these are completely out of our control, there *are* times that have been dictated by others that we can challenge.

Some of us can get into time habits, for instance getting up in the morning. We tend to get up at the same time, do the same things in the same order and take roughly the same amount of time to do them. Very often, we haven't consciously thought about it, we just do it this way because we always have. Sometimes it pays to challenge time habits, whether good or bad, simply to see if we are actually making the best use of our time and if we are doing the right task at the right time, both at home and at work.

Daily Time Log

A daily time log can help you to establish exactly on what you are spending your time. This knowledge helps you to understand what amounts of time you are allocating to your 'time mortgage' and what amounts to your 'time new frock or suit', in the same way that you might look at your bank statement to see on what and when you spent your money.

Analysing a time log can help you to identify areas where you might save time, or areas that are clearly time wasting.

It is a good idea to do a time log for your total day, not just work, so that you can see if you are spending enough time, for example, with your family.

Example of a Life Time Log

Time	Activity	No of minutes
0700	Got up, washed and showered	10
0710	Ate breakfast	15
0725	Dressed (ironed jacket)	20
0745	Drove to station - listened to the news	15
0800	Arrived station, stood on platform in rain	15
0815	Train arrived – read paper	20
0835	Fell asleep	15
0850	Woke up – arrived at station, walked to work	10
0900	Arrived at work, got coffee from machine, chatted to Millie	15
0915	Began opening post	7
0922	Interrupted by Fred re invoice	18
0940	Back to opening post	15
0955	Phone call – Margaret re Jon Evans	13
1008	Back to opening post	12
1020	Manager rang re meeting tomorrow	10
1030	Finished off opening post	15
1045	Stopped for coffee – met Robin by machine mentioned tomorrow's meeting	13
1058	Phoned George re XYZ Co	13
*****	******************************	**********
1735	Caught train – fell asleep	35
1810	Arrived station – drove home, listened to radio	15
1825	Arrived home, said hi to F and kids	5
1830	Washed and changed	15
1845	Started preparing dinner	17
1902	Mum rang	28
1930	Finished preparing dinner	15
1945	Laid table	5
1950	Sat down to eat with F & kids	15
2010	Miriam rang, interrupted dinner – said I'd ring back	2
2012	Finished dinner	16
2028	Cleared table and washed dishes	17
2045	Rang Miriam back – just gossiped	15
2100	Watched news	30
2130	Finished off report for tomorrow's meeting	40
2210	Chased kids to bed	10
2220	Watched rest of Newsnight	25
2245	Got ready for bed	15
2300	Went to sleep!	

Having done this you can start to re-think and re-plan your priorities. Then you can begin to use time in the way **you** want to, not in the way other people dictate.

Checklist

- Remember that time is a valuable commodity. There is a limited amount.
- Calculate how much time you have available and what you want to spend it on.
- Identify your 'time mortgages' and your 'time new frocks'.
- Challenge your time habits.
- Do a daily life time log.

Planning and Prioritising by Objectives

Time is like money in that we have a certain amount of it that we need to budget and re-budget in order to get the best use out of it.

At work, you are judged by the outcomes you produce, based on what is expected of you. There are certain things that you have to do as part of your job that aren't necessarily directly linked to what you are measured on. For example, you may have to attend meetings, but attendance at meetings is not what you are appraised on at the end of the year. *"Well done, Caroline, you didn't meet budget, but you did attend 405 meetings this year!"* is not a comment you are likely to hear your manager make.

There are various different kinds of tasks that we get involved in at work. Some of them are important, and not carrying them out could result in our losing our jobs. Some are not so important, but have to be done because they are part of internal procedures, some of them are relatively unimportant and could be done by somebody else and some aren't important at all and don't need to be done. We do them simply because that particular piece of paper landed on our desk and we feel we ought to.

Learning to differentiate amongst the different kinds of tasks that you are expected to carry out at work is the first step towards planning and prioritising effectively. The same is true at home. There are some jobs that absolutely have to be done, e.g., cooking and washing up. There are others that you don't **have** to do, you just do because you want to, like clearing out the attic perhaps.

All of us, despite doing different jobs, are working towards the organisation's objectives. Essentially, all job objectives fit into the objectives of the department and the overall objectives of the organisation. You should be absolutely sure that you know the overall objectives of both your organisation and your department. Write them down and then check them with your manager.

Identifying 'time mortgages'

When you joined your organisation you were given a job description which detailed the areas that you are account-able for. Your job description should be updated at least once a year and the information contained within it will normally be your 'time mortgage'. In other words, the objectives and/or tasks outlined on your job description are the ones that your organisation pays you to achieve.

They must be achieved in order to fulfil the terms of your contract of employment. They are your 'time mortgages'.

If you don't have a job description, then write one of your own detailing what you think the key areas of your job are. Take this to your manager to check if that tallies with what he or she thinks your job is. You might get some surprises!

Similarly, if you are accountable for a team who don't have job descriptions, or at least ones that are up to date, then you should ask them to write their own and discuss it with you.

It is much more effective to get the person actually carrying out the job to write the job summary/description as they know the job in more detail than you do.

What a job summary/description should contain

A job summary is essentially an informal version of a job description. A job description is a written statement of what the employee is expected to do within the organisation. It should:

- establish a common understanding of the content of the job between the job holder and the manager
- describe the job
- set realistic and agreed job responsibilities, making clear the relationship between jobs to avoid overlapping and gaps
- clarify functions and responsibilities
- provide the job holder with the nature, scope and content of the job

- provide a definition of the organisation's expectations of the job holder.

Job Objectives

Begin by writing down what you believe the main objectives of your job are. Make sure that as you are writing them you are comparing them to the overall objectives of both the organisation and your department. Remember that an *objective* differs from a *task* in that a *task describes the action that needs to be taken* whereas *an objective describes the end results*.

For example, your objective might be to achieve sales of £50,000 during the financial year. That is the *objective*. What you do to *gain* that £50,000 are the specific tasks that you do.

Normally a job has one overall objective with between 5–8 Key Result Areas. A Key Result Area is, in a sense, a slightly more detailed objective. See the example overleaf.

Overall objective: To manage the Research and Development Team to produce new products for the organisation to help to maintain and increase income.

Key Result Areas

1   To organise and plan research and development within the budget limits and to the organisation needs.
2   To manage and motivate a team of six people to achieve this.
3   To create additional income of £x amount during the financial year.
4   To get funding of £y per year for the ABC product development.
5   To liaise with key customers to try out new products on our behalf.

The next step is to break the Key Result Areas into lists of tasks that specifically relate to the achievement of those Key Result Areas. See overleaf.

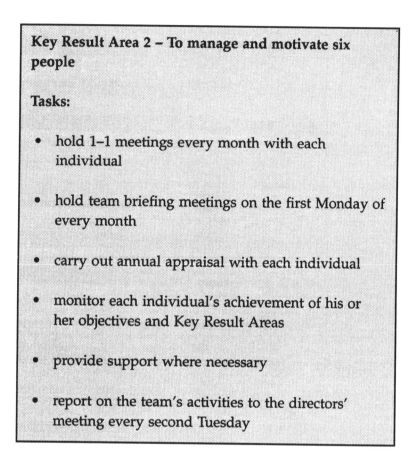

Key Result Area 2 – To manage and motivate six people

Tasks:

- hold 1–1 meetings every month with each individual

- hold team briefing meetings on the first Monday of every month

- carry out annual appraisal with each individual

- monitor each individual's achievement of his or her objectives and Key Result Areas

- provide support where necessary

- report on the team's activities to the directors' meeting every second Tuesday

All the above tasks need to be carried out in order to meet the Key Result Area.

- Write down for yourself your own overall job objectives and your Key Result Areas (even if you already have a job description – jobs do change)
- Speak to your manager about them

You have now identified your job objectives and Key Result Areas. These are your 'time mortgages' and will normally take priority during the working day and week as tasks that absolutely must be achieved.

Reactive and Proactive Tasks

There is a very simple approach to time and workload management. It's **LITRW** which stands for **Live in the Real World.**

In the real world things go wrong, computers break down. People behave in ways you don't expect. Paperwork is delayed, trains run late. Managers are unreasonable and impatient. Accept that there are certain things that you cannot change, but you *can* change the way in which you manage the real world in which you live.

You will probably recognise two different kinds of people at work. There is the kind who are always rushing about, missing deadlines, generally seeming panicked and disorganised. Then there are those who seem calm and unflurried, meet deadlines and always seem to have time to talk to people and get jobs done. The only difference is that the second sort of person manages and organises himself or herself effectively.

Time and workload management is about self discipline. It is not the *system* that makes the difference (although, of course, systems can help) it is whether or not you *stick* to the system you have chosen in a disciplined way.

Most tasks can be broken down into *reactive* and *proactive*. Reactive tasks are generally those tasks which are immediate whilst proactive tasks are those that we can plan for in advance. You need to identify roughly what proportion of your working life (normally in days or weeks) is on average reactive or proactive. Clearly it varies during the year, but you do need to have some kind of an idea. For example, when you think about it you may find that 70% of your job is reactive and 30% is proactive. Whatever the percentages are, this is your real world and you need to live in it. If you know that usually 50% of your day is spent dealing with reactive tasks that you couldn't have anticipated, then when planning that day, you need to leave yourself with four hours with nothing to do. Because the reality is that those four hours will fill up with reactive tasks.

Most people have a tendency to plan for 100% proactive time in a working day. Unfortunately, this is never achieved because reactive tasks **always** crop up and have to be dealt with. Plan for things to go wrong, for you to be interrupted, for your manager to have a crisis. You are then much more likely to achieve at least those proactive tasks that you had planned to do.

Most of us have had the experience when at school or college of having been given two weeks to do our homework, then leaving it to the last minute, or doing it on the bus on the way into school, which normally resulted in homework not being of the calibre it could or should have been.

Similarly, at work, if you leave things to the last minute then you must expect that you won't do a good job. If you leave things to do on the day of your deadline then Murphy's law says that the computer will break down, or you'll be late for work, or there'll be a crisis that you have to deal with. Leaving things to the last minute is asking for trouble. You will get very little sympathy for missing a deadline that you had plenty of time to achieve, regardless of the validity of the argument that says you had too many other things to do as well.

Don't leave things to the last minute. At the very least, do the work a couple of days before it is due. That way if something *does* go wrong, you have left yourself some leeway.

Checklist

- Write or up-date your job summary/description.
- Get your team to do the same.
- Write down the main objectives of your job, then identify your Key Result Areas.
- Write down the important tasks that will help you to achieve your Key Result Areas.
- Work out your proactive and reactive time.
- Allow time for things to go wrong.
- Live in The Real World.

Task Management

One of the most underused tools that we have available to us at work is the diary. Most of us keep a diary of some description. Often it's a small pocket diary that Aunt Maud gives us every Christmas and in which we keep notes of birthdays, holidays and the odd appointment. A diary can be used to much better effect.

A typical example of a diary looks like this:

	Monday	**Tuesday**	**Wednesday**	**Thursday**	**Friday**
0800		Day off	Doctor's appointment		
0900					1–1 Sue
1000	Team meeting			Appraisal: Robert	
1100					
1200	Lunch: Fred				
1300				Planning meeting	Team lunch
1400			1–1 Mike		
1500	Meeting				Directors' meeting
1600	John Johnson				
1700					
1800			Dinner party Carol & Tom		

The diary is used as a reminder of meetings that we need to attend and sometimes things that we don't want to forget. However, according to our example diary we are doing nothing in between the meetings, appointments etc. Of course, that isn't true. What we are in fact doing is **our job.**

By writing meetings and appointments into our diaries, we are basically committing our time to other people. What we may not be so good at is committing time to ourselves. We need more time to ourselves than we give to others because we have a job to do in addition to all the meetings that we have to attend.

A more effective way of using the diary is to plan in time or make appointments to carry out tasks. This will help you to manage your reactive and proactive time more effectively and allow you to build in time in a realistic and workable way for things to go wrong. If you have a report to do that's due on Thursday lunchtime, do the report on Tuesday and give yourself a full day spare in case something should crop up or go wrong.

In the ideal world the report might take you one hour to complete. In the Real World, you need to allow one and a half hours – in case of interruptions or something going wrong.

In your diary make an appointment at 2 pm to write the report. Don't schedule the next task until 3.30 pm. If all goes well and you complete the report without interruptions you will have gained half an hour in your diary to do something else with. Even if you are interrupted, you are much more likely to have achieved the task within the deadline that you set for yourself.

Given the opportunity to estimate how much time a job is going to take, people will nearly always underestimate. Using a diary in this way will help you to make more sensible decisions about how to allocate time to others and agree to deadlines that you can realistically meet without affecting the rest of your work.

Example

	Monday	Tuesday	Wednesday	Thursday	Friday
0800		Day off	Doctor's appointment		
0900	Prepare for team meeting		Admin time	Prepare for Robert's appraisal	1-1 Sue
1000	Team meeting			Appraisal: Robert	Finish budget
1100					
1200	Lunch: Fred		Write monthly report	Write up Rob's appraisal	
1300				Planning meeting	Team lunch
1400	Prepare for Robert's appraisal		1-1 Mike		Directors' meeting
1500	Meeting John Johnson				
1600				Prepare papers for Directors' meeting	Leave to go to Tom's play
1700					
1800			Dinner party Carol & Tom		

Rolling to do lists

A rolling to do list is a book which is dated, or a page in your diary. Instead of writing down a daily list of things to do, or a weekly one and moving things from one list to the other, you write down what you have to do on the day on which you **intend to do it.** This is similar to making appointments in your diary to do tasks, except that in your diary you make appointments to do big jobs (normally ones that will take you half an hour or more) whereas the rolling to do list contains small, fairly quick jobs, e.g., telephone a customer, check an invoice, write a letter, etc.

For example, today is Wednesday 16th and you get a phone call from a colleague asking you to do something. You aren't going to do it today or immediately, because you don't have to, so you turn to a page in your diary when you can do it (let's say the 22nd) and write it down there.

You can then completely forget about your colleague's request, because when you open your diary or dated book on the 22nd, you will see it written there and that will remind you to do it. Don't have more than eight things planned for any one day. Generally, you won't be able to complete more than eight, and the consequences of not completing your to do list will lead to feelings of under-achievement and stress.

There are no hard and fast rules. You will frequently find yourself re-arranging diary appointments and to-dos as things crop up. However, you will never forget what things need to be done and you will be constantly planning for when you can do them.

Ideally, you need a diary that is big enough to take both

your appointments and your rolling to do list. This reduces the number of books that you have to check in order to see what you have planned for the day.

An A5 page to a day or A4 page to a day is ideal. Alternatively, there are many other kinds of diaries on the market which will give you enough room to write in both appointments and your to-dos for that day.

THURSDAY 16 NOVEMBER	TO DO TODAY
0900 *Prepare for Robert's appraisal*	• check last year's income budget • re-arrange 1–1 with Mike for next Wednesday
1000 Robert's appraisal	• Buy thank you card for Carol & Tom
1100	• Has MSP returned my call?
1200 *Write up Robert's appraisal*	• Have you heard from Jim re PDP?
1300 Planning meeting	• Check we've received cheque from DTI
1400	• Agenda for next week's team briefing meeting
1500	
1600 *Prepare papers for Directors' meeting*	
1700	
1800	
1900	

Managing deadlines

Every day at work you are either setting or agreeing to deadlines. Deadlines matter and everyone has them. Nearly every job has a deadline set against it.

Some deadlines are obvious and occur because the job needs to happen by such and such a date in order for something else to happen. For example, departmental monthly accounts need to be in by the end of every month so that the accounts department can work out how well the whole organisation is doing. Other deadlines are arbitrary. For example, sorting out the filing cabinets. It may be that you set a deadline which seems achievable, but where if you can't do it it doesn't actually matter all that much.

The main problems with deadlines is that we are either totally unrealistic, or we agree to them without really thinking through the implications. Imagine that you have been asked by your manager or a customer to meet a deadline. You protest at the deadline because you know you won't be able to meet it. However, your manager or the customer is determined, and you end up agreeing to the deadline, knowing full well that there is no way you can meet it, or at least suspecting that you won't be able to. You may even add the rider "I'll try", but essentially you have agreed to the deadline in order to keep your manager or your customer happy.

Then, as you **knew** you would, you miss the deadline. Your manager or customer won't remember that you protested the deadline in the beginning. What they *will* remember is that you didn't meet the deadline – that you made a commitment which you failed to keep.

So, how do you manage to agree a deadline that is realistic without alienating your manager or your customer?

- Instead of giving a deadline that you know you can't meet, stand your ground.
- Explain the exact reason why you can't meet that particular deadline (explaining what it is that prevents you).
- Offer an alternative deadline that you *can* meet.

This way, although at the time you may appear to be being slightly unco-operative, you will meet the deadline – and that is what your manager or your customer will remember. You will then get a reputation for being someone who meets deadlines, which makes it more likely that others will meet *your* deadlines.

General guidelines for managing deadlines

- Whenever you are asked to agree to a deadline, check first in your diary/rolling to do list whether you can realistically set aside time to do the work that will enable you to meet that deadline.
- Never use the words 'as soon as possible'. They don't mean anything to anyone. If you have a lot of paperwork all marked as soon as possible, you don't know what order to do it in, so you just do whatever you fancy. Always give people a **specific** date and time with a **reason** for the deadline. (Tell them what the consequences are of not meeting that deadline, for example. Even senior people and customers appreciate that.)
- When you receive something marked as soon as possible, telephone the sender to find out when you **actually** need to do it by.
- Similar rules apply to the word 'URGENT'. How urgent is 'urgent'? You have no way of knowing. So, again, give a

specific date and time, with reasons/consequences of the deadline not being met. If you receive something marked urgent, ring and check when it's really needed by.

■ When sending out paperwork that you wish returned or replied to, always give a deadline for your response and where necessary a reason for the deadline.

■ When leaving telephone messages, give a deadline for the action you need and why the deadline exists.

■ Never leave it to the last minute to chase someone if there is a deadline. You **know** that you haven't received whatever it was and that it's likely that it hasn't been done. By chasing at the time of the deadline, you are setting the scene for you to get angry and the other person to get defensive.

■ Write a note of when you need to chase someone prior to the deadline in your rolling to do list.

■ When setting deadlines, let people know that you will be chasing them in advance of the deadline. You can do it politely by saying something like *"I'll ring you on Tuesday to see how you're getting on/if there are any problems etc"*. Very few people will be offended by that. They are much more likely to welcome it.

Checklist

■ Plan appointments in your diary to do tasks.
■ Use a rolling to do list.
■ Don't agree to deadlines you know you can't meet.
■ Don't use as soon as possible or URGENT – always give specific deadlines.

Workload Management Systems

The key to effective time and workload management is not so much about systems as self discipline. Systems do help of course and this chapter is dedicated to suggesting systems you could implement at work which may help you to be more effective.

Dealing with paperwork effectively

There are some bad habits to do with paperwork that you will do instinctively without thinking, for example, looking through each piece of post before dealing with it. This means that you will have read or glanced at each piece of paper at least twice before you even do anything with it.

Other bad paperwork habits include:

- throwing paper into a pending tray where it festers for days, if not weeks
- keeping every piece and throwing few away
- replying to letters and memos that don't need replies
- keeping copies of internal memos and reports
- having your desk littered with all the bits of paper that you are working on
- sending one line typed replies to internal memos
- moving pieces of paper from one tray to another – and then back again
- putting things to one side that you are not sure how to deal with and looking at them several times before you then file them
- not throwing paper away
- having more than one place where you keep current paperwork, e.g., on the desk, in a drawer, in a pending tray, in your in-tray, in your action tray so that you're never quite sure where any piece of paper is when you need it
- sending memos when a phone call would do

The thing about paper is that the more of it we produce, the more we will feel we are "producing", or "being effective at work". Of course, this is not the case and on the whole the amount of paperwork we produce is usually in inverse proportion to how effective we are at our jobs.

If you are a manager, your primary job is to manage and motivate the people who work within your team. You don't manage people through bits of paper, you manage them by talking to them, going to see them at their place of work, even if it's only their desk two feet away from yours! If you're tied up dealing with paperwork you won't be managing your team.

To be effective you need to reduce the amount of paperwork that you have to deal with to give you more time to spend talking to people.

The Post

- Find a time during the day that really is the best time for you to deal with the post. It may be that this *isn't* as soon as it arrives. Of course, there may be something important in there. However, experience shows that usually even important letters in the post can wait a few hours. If it really *is* urgent it would be faxed.
- Make opening the post a regular time each day.
- As you open the post deal with each piece of paper as you touch it. **Do not** look through it to see what's there. This wastes valuable time and can also distract you into dealing with something that could wait rather than tackling something that needs dealing with there and then.
- If the piece of paper you have picked up requires relatively quick action (e.g., dictating a reply or making a phone call) then do it there and then. If you can't do it there and then, put it into the Bring Forward to deal with later (The bring forward system is discussed later in this chapter).
- If you can take some action on the piece of paper, but not complete it, then take the action you can take and put the paper into the bring forward system or a note in your rolling to do list as to when you can finish off the action.

- If the paper is for reading and is less than one side of A4, read it immediately and THROW IT AWAY.
- If it's longer than a piece of A4 then diary time to read it or put a note in your rolling to do list. However, be honest with yourself. Will you **really** ever read it, even though you'd like to and think you might get round to it one day? Pending trays and filing cabinets are littered with the documents that we thought we might read one day (normally ten years out of date!) If you know, deep down, that in reality that you are unlikely to read it, then either throw it away or give it to someone who might have the time to read it.
- If it is junk then put it straight into the bin.
- Do not keep any paper unless it is absolutely necessary.

If it's an internal memo that requires a reply – don't dictate or type a reply. Write your response (legibly) at the bottom of the memo and send the original back to the originator. Normally, you shouldn't need to keep a copy, but if you do then photocopy it.

Example

Memorandum

To: Ginny *John*
From: John *Ginny*
Date: *18 November*
Subject: *Early retirement party*

Ginny,

As you know, Mike Harris retires early at the end of this month. I would like to pay out of my budget for a retirement party for 100 people at the Sports & Social club to honour his leaving. Certainly, Mike has done a sterling job for us and I do think we should show our appreciation. I also think it would be good morale for the rest of the team and other staff in the company.

Total cost estimated to be around £2000. (This includes all booze and food.) Can I go ahead?

John, go ahead. Please make sure you invite the MD. £2000 seems a bit steep though. Find out how much one round of sparkling wine or reasonable champagne is and we'll pay for that. People can buy their own drinks at the bar. It's subsidised anyway.

The Bring Forward System

A bring forward system is a concertina file or drawer with lateral filing sections numbered 1–31 (representing the days in the month). Put in it any written material that you need to see appear on your desk on any given day. Perhaps you wrote a letter to a customer on the 12th and you want a reply by the 20th. Put a copy of the letter or a note into the bring forward system in the section marked 20. Every day you pull out of the bring forward system all the paper in that slot for that particular day, in that month. When you come to the 20th you retrieve the copy of the letter to the customer and check if you have received a reply.

The main advantage of the bring forward system is that you no longer need a pending tray. Any papers that you aren't working on at the moment either go into the normal filing system or into the bring forward system. If you need the paper before the day it's due look through the slots around the time to which you think you will have brought it forward.

You can use a bring forward system for:

- letters requiring an answer
- reminders for deadlines
- reports and papers
- items for agendas
- telephone calls to be made
- follow up action reminders
- reminders about appointments/birthdays
- monitoring delegation
- notes for 1-1s with members of your team

Trays

Have only two trays on your desk, an in tray and an out tray. If you are using a bring forward system properly you won't need any other trays.

The In tray should be emptied at least twice a day. If you are someone who always has an overflowing in tray, you will tend to find that people put paper in the middle of your desk because they want to make sure that you've seen it.

People *will* put things into your in tray if they can see that it is emptied regularly. You don't have to deal with the paperwork straightaway. You can put it into the bring forward system to deal with on another occasion. If people are confident that you have taken it out of the in tray and seen it then they will trust that you will deal with it and not chase you for it.

Filing

If you either do your own filing or have someone else to do the filing for you, the only rule is DO IT EVERY DAY, then you will only have a few pieces of paper to file at a time. If you leave it to collect, it grows into a paper mountain which you know will take hours to file so you won't do it!

Filing is normally best done as one of the routine chores (like dealing with the post) first thing in the morning. This way, it becomes a habit.

Movement sheets

If you or your team spend time out of the office, produce weekly movement sheets. A weekly movement sheet gives basic details of where people are on any given day at any given time, usually with a contact number. Movement sheets should be produced weekly and circulated to all those people who will find it useful.

Movement sheets save a lot of time when customers or other people ring the office looking for a particular person. It is so much quicker and more professional to be able to look at the movement sheet and tell the caller where the individual is and what time he or she is expected back.

Example

	Mon 18	Tue 19	Wed 20	Thu 21	Fri 22
Mark	office	am – Visit: J Jones & Co (Tel.) pm office	am – team meeting pm office	am – 1-1 Jean pm – visit ABC Co (Tel.)	am – office pm half day hols
Jean	office	office	am – team meeting	am – 1-1 Mark	meeting in Leeds office all day
Michael	Sales course – Manchester all day (Tel.)	office	am – team meeting, pm – office	am – visit T Maxim (Tel.) 12.30 – 2.00 lunch Tom Mikes pm – office	meeting in Leeds office all day
Elizabeth	Hols	Hols	Hols	Hols	Hols

Everything book

An everything book is an A4 hardback book that you keep with you at all times. Anything at all that you have to write down, from minutes of meetings to scribbling telephone numbers whilst on the telephone, is written into this one book. You will never have to hunt around for that scrap of paper on which you wrote that really important telephone message and when others see you are writing notes they will assume you will take action and not bother you with unnecessary reminders. *If you have a secretary, see chapter 9, Working with a Secretary, for tips on how to use your secretary to help you to manage paperwork.*

Checklist

- Deal with paperwork immediately.
- Implement a bring forward system.
- Throw paper away.
- Only have two trays – in and out.
- File every day.
- Use movement sheets.
- Use an Everything book.

Ruthless with Time – Kind to People

Most of the jobs that we do at work involve getting results through other people. This particularly applies to those with a management role.

Everyday at work we deal with people: colleagues, members of our team, customers, managers more senior to us. Every interaction with them that we have influences both our ability and theirs to get jobs done in the most effective and efficient way.

Good time and workload management is not about shutting yourself away in your office for four days to plough through your paperwork. It is about building relationships with people, where you are trusted to play your part and they are trusted to play theirs. This includes people external to the organisation.

You can probably think of examples of when your behaviour, or that of another person, has had an adverse effect on your ability to achieve results. Similarly, you must be able to think of a time when your behaviour, or someone else's, has actually helped you to get better results.

The time that you spend briefly chatting with a colleague at the photocopier or coffee machine is not necessarily time wasted. By taking the time to talk to people and build up relationships, we are creating an atmosphere of mutual co-operation and support. Provided the chatting about seemingly inconsequential things is not taken to excess, it is, surprisingly, a valuable time-management tool.

Getting to know people

It is a truism that we will expend more time and energy helping our friends than we ever will our enemies. This is a fact of life, and no amount of saying "he or she **should** do something" is ever going to change that.

So one of our priorities at work should be to build up effective working relationships with our colleagues, the people we need to help us to do our job.

Take the following actions to begin to build up better working relationships with others at work:

- Get to know other people face to face. Visit them in their own departments.
- Instead of always sending things in the internal post, take it round yourself to create an opportunity to see people.
- Whenever you visit another department, make an effort to speak to at least one or two people. Always greet them cheerfully.

- Smile and thank people if they do something for you, even if it's small and part of their job anyway.
- If you see someone from another department visiting your own, make an effort to greet them and offer them refreshments.
- Find out exactly what other departments do. Take an interest in their work.
- All departments are important in an organisation; it is rare to find one more important than another. Make sure you acknowledge the importance of other people's work.
- Find out what other department's/people's problems are. See if you can find something that can be done in your department to make their lives easier. (With accounts, for example, you could make sure your expenses are in on time.)
- Stick to your deadlines. If you have a problem, let other people concerned know well in advance.
- Be honest without being unhelpful or impolite. If you can't help someone, say so, give the reasons and offer alternative suggestions.
- When people visit your department, make an effort to introduce them to members of your team.

Managing Behaviour

To get understanding, co-operation and commitment from others begin from where *they* are. In any situation, imagine what it might be like to walk in the other person's shoes. If you begin any interaction with that thought you will find it a lot easier to deal with people in a way that gets results. You will understand what is motivating and influencing their behaviour and you can adjust yours accordingly. This is not manipulative, it is common sense. You would probably like someone to see things from your point of view whenever they are dealing with you.

Understanding behaviour

The outcome of any situation is dependent on how you choose to behave. The old saying, "behaviour breeds behaviour" is very true.

When dealing with people you will normally be doing one of two things: initiating or responding. How you initiate and how you respond will have a major impact on whether or not you get the result you are looking for.

Imagine that people are like onions, made up of layers, and that each layer represents a certain part of us. The core of the onion is where our personal values lie. These are the values that were taught to us as a child and we are very unlikely to ever be able to change them. Often we are not even aware that they exist because they are buried deep in our subconscious. Nonetheless, they have a major impact on the way in which we live our lives and deal with the people we come into contact with.

The second layer is our attitudes and beliefs. These are formed out of our values. Attitude is what or how you think about a particular thing. You like classical music for example, or you dislike people who are loud.

The third layer is that of our feelings. Our feelings are strongly influenced by our attitudes. To take the previous examples, if you like classical music, when you hear it you will feel good. If you dislike loud people, when you hear them you will feel irritated or angry.

The final and top layer is our behaviour. Our behaviour comes directly from our feelings. If we feel good, we smile. If we feel angry, we frown. If we like someone, we are kind to them; if we dislike them, we ignore them, and so on.

The only thing we can really deal with is the behaviour. We need to understand where that behaviour is coming from in order to choose the most appropriate behaviour ourselves.

If, for example, you call someone into your office to tell them off about something, such as missing a deadline, you may find their behaviour slightly hostile and defensive. This is natural, because they are possibly feeling threatened and this is bound to reflect in their behaviour. If, however, you recognise where this behaviour is coming from you can adjust yours to get the result. So, knowing that they are feeling threatened, you can take steps to reassure them by behaving in an appropriate way.

In any situation the way that you behave is what others will see and respond to. However, you may not always be aware of the other person's values, attitudes and feelings which underpin the behaviour that you see. For example, it may be that you have had a bad morning. You missed the bus, and the first thing a colleague says to you is "You're late." You will probably respond aggressively and snap "I know, I do have a watch."

We make up our minds about most things very quickly, certainly about people, and on the whole human beings are a very unforgiving race. If someone has annoyed or hurt us in the past, that will influence our whole view of that person, and no matter what they do or say we are likely to view them with prejudice. This will affect our behaviour towards them. We have made our mind up about them and so we are unlikely to listen *properly* to them. We will listen with prejudice rather than with an open mind.

You should aim for a result without hurting, embarrassing or making another person feel bad. Even if in the short term you get what you want, and at the same time give vent to your feelings, in the long run you will have damaged the relationship and find it harder to get results next time.

How to behave

In any communication situation there are three first steps.

Step One   **Stop**: assess the situation, examine your own attitude

Step Two   **Look**: at the other person, what are they telling you through their body language and expression?

Step Three **Listen:** without prejudice. What are they trying to tell you?

By following these three steps you have begun by trying to put yourself in the other person's shoes. You have understood his or her point of view, needs and feelings.

Now you can state your side of things, honestly and clearly and say what you would like to happen.

It is important to show people empathy. It shows that you are not dismissing the other person or his or her situation. This does not mean that you cannot still clearly state your needs, but you have done so in a way that has left the other person feeling OK and has protected your relationship.

To respond to situations that you are unhappy with use the following formula:

When you ....

I feel/x happens ....

I'd like ....

Example

Mike, *when you* interrupt me while I'm writing my report
I feel frustrated and irritated because *it means* I can't concentrate
I'd prefer if you waited to talk to me until you could see I am finished.

Always make sure that you focus on the future, not on the past. What's happened has happened and you can't undo it. So there is no point dwelling on it. It is much more effective to concentrate on avoiding the same thing happening in the future.

When making requests
- be direct and to the point
- explain why you are making the request
- explain the importance/consequences of the request not being met
- keep it short
- don't manipulate
- don't personalise the request
- be prepared for refusal

Refusing requests

- show empathy
- say 'no' simply, clearly and directly
- avoid profuse apologies
- explain, don't justify
- keep it short
- don't personalise
- use repetition if your original 'no' isn't getting through
- offer alternative solutions if you can

Information gathering

- explain why you require the information
- avoid over-justification
- ask open questions
- listen
- don't interrupt
- don't feel the need to respond verbally to every statement the other person makes

Information giving

- state your objectives
- be direct and to the point
- avoid over-justification
- summarise
- explain what action you want and why
- listen

Disagreeing

- clearly identify areas of agreement first
- then clearly and objectively identify the areas of disagreement
- listen

- show that you understand the other person's view
- don't personalise the disagreement
- disagree with what is said, not the person saying it
- be prepared to change your opinion
- negotiate a positive solution

Checklist

- Get to know people in other departments.
- Spend time building up relationships.
- Start from where the other person is.
- Think about what is influencing both your behaviour and the other person's behaviour.
- Stop – Look – Listen.
- Use the "When you . . . I feel . . . . . I'd like . . . . ." formula.

Managing Interruptions

Interruptions are one of the major causes of wasted time at work. There are several kinds of interruptions:

- useful/essential
- useful/could have waited
- not useful
- ones caused by yourself

Interruptions are a big problem area. You will never be able to eliminate them entirely. However, there are certain actions you can take to minimise and control them.

Part of the problem is our own perception of and attitude towards interruptions. When we are interrupted we tend to stop what we are doing to talk to the interrupter, and we end up dealing with something that we hadn't planned on dealing with at that time. It also encourages people to continue interrupting because they know that we will respond.

You are not the only person who suffers when you allow yourself to be interrupted and diverted from what you were working on. It has a knock on effect on the rest of the team.

Being available

You probably have a perception that you must always be available, especially if you are a manager. It is not the case. You take holidays, attend meetings, go to the dentist, pop out of the office to interrupt someone else! During that time, life carries on. If you want to know how indispensable you are, stick your hand into a bucket of water and see what the effect is when you take it out. Is there a gaping hole? In fact, being indispensable is actually very career limiting, because no one will promote you out of a department that will collapse if you're not there.

People will interrupt you much less if you tell them a time when you are, or are not, available. You don't know who will interrupt you, but you can guarantee that someone will and can plan your workload accordingly. People will also register when you are and aren't available and will only interrupt you when they know you will be in and receptive to them.

- Set aside time in your diary when you are available to see anyone without an appointment. Make it the same time each week if possible.
- At all other times, make it clear that you won't see people who don't have an appointment.

- Allow your secretary, if you have one, to make decisions about who can and can't interrupt you.

Dealing with telephone interruptions

The telephone is the most usual form of interruption. We do it to others and they do it to us. We assume that the person at the other end of the phone has time to talk to us there and then. And we assume that because we have picked up the phone we should talk to them.

- Make telephone appointments. If you plan to ring someone, tell them (or whoever takes the message) the specific time you will be calling. If you receive a message saying that someone will be phoning you at 3pm, you are much more likely to be at your desk then.
- If you are asking someone to call you back, give them a specific time when you will be available. They are then more likely to return your call when it's convenient for you. They are also more likely to actually return your call!
- Don't play telephone tag – returning your call returning their call returning your call! Make a specific time.
- If you telephone someone and they're not available, retain control of your time. Offer to ring them back at a specific time. This way you control when you interrupt your work and not the other person.
- Learn the facilities that your telephone has to offer.
- When you call someone, the first thing you should say is what you are calling about, how much of his or her time you think you need and whether it is convenient for them to speak to you now. If it isn't, offer to call back when it is.

- Before making the call, prepare a brief telephone agenda – a few points that you want to cover, and tick off each point as you do.
- Keep a note of actions agreed on the telephone in the everything book and transfer to your rolling to do list, bring forward or diary once the call is completed.
- Use telephone message forms and encourage the people you work with to do the same. If people are required to fill in specific forms, the questions on the form will prompt them to take down the message correctly.
- Use message boards – baize boards with people's names on and spaces underneath to pin messages. People will automatically look at the board as soon as they come into the office (they won't be able to help themselves). Also it saves time when people ring in if you are out of the office, as whoever takes the call can simply pull the messages off the board and read them over the phone.

Example telephone message form

Telephone Message	
TO	**TIME**
FROM	**DATE**
COMPANY	**TAKEN BY**
	EXTN
TELEPHONE NO	
MESSAGE	
□ Please ring back □ Returned your call □ Will ring back □ When available	

Time-to-Think periods

A time-to-think period is the equivalent to having an office door which when closed means Do Not Disturb.

Agree with your team/colleagues a rota of time when each of you is protected from phone calls and visitors by the others. If anyone wants you, your colleagues simply take messages for you. To work this there needs to be a reciprocal arrangement and at a regular time each week. You also need to make sure that you don't interrupt your colleagues yourself!

General tips to avoid interruptions

■ Don't be an interrupter yourself
■ Meet deadlines

- Make as many requests as you can on paper to avoid interrupting others (the paper doesn't have to be typed)
- Be seen to write down actions that you have agreed to take
- Keep a clear desk and clean in tray so people don't feel they have to interrupt you to make sure that something they wanted you to do has been done
- Be firm and polite with interrupters. If you can't speak to them now, say so, say why and say when you *can* speak to them.

Checklist

- Set aside time when you are and are not available.
- Make telephone appointments.
- Use telephone message forms.
- Use telephone message boards.
- Have 'time-to-think' periods.
- Don't interrupt others.

Delegation

Delegation is a word that is frequently misunderstood and used in the wrong context. If work comes into the department and you dish it out, that is NOT delegation, it's *allocation*. Delegation is when you deliberately choose to give a member of your team the authority to carry out a piece of work that you would normally do *yourself*, that is part of *your* job description and that *you* are paid to do.

Every job is made up of three levels:

Responsibility This is the "doing" part of the job. If you are responsible for writing a report then you are the person who actually writes it.

Authority This is the "decision-making" part of the job. If you have authority with responsibility then you decide how the job is done.

For example, with the report, you decide how you present it, what language you use, what format it is in and so on.

Accountability This is the "who carries the can" part of the job. If you are accountable, then no matter who actually carries out the task you retain full accountability for it if it goes wrong.

Successful delegation is matching responsibility with authority. You have not delegated if you give someone responsibility for a job without also giving him or her authority to make decisions as to how he or she does the job.

As a manager, you will always retain accountability. If you delegate a job to a member of your team and he or she makes a mistake it will be your job to own that mistake.

Commonly Perceived Risks and Problems Associated with Delegating

- quicker to do it yourself
- no one has the skills or ability
- they might get it wrong
- they might do it better
- you haven't got the time to train them
- they already have too much to do
- they might think you're dumping on them
- you might do yourself out of a job
- loss of control

All the risks and problems associated above are real feelings. However, delegation is important and is in fact part of the job of a manager. Most management courses include sessions on delegation and most organisations want their managers to delegate.

Why delegate? – Benefits of delegation

- Delegation enables you to concentrate on those aspects of your job which require personal experience, skill and knowledge.
- Most of a manager's job should be focused on planning the future rather than organising the present.
- Managers should also be concentrating on enabling others to do, not doing themselves.
- Delegation is good for motivation.
- Delegation is a way of training people.
- It is cheaper and more cost effective for an organisation to have its managers delegating work to people on a lower salary.
- It is good for career development of your staff.

The Delegation Process

In order to ensure that you minimise the risks and maximise the benefits of delegation, there are a series of steps that you need to carry out.

Before

- Look at your Key Result Areas and other tasks that you have to carry out.
- Choose a number of tasks that you could delegate on the basis of the following questions:
  - Do I have to do this task?

- Why do I do it?
- Should I keep it and why?
- Who else could do this job?
- Who should I be training up to do it?

- What are the consequences of delegating this particular task?
- Assess the willingness of the individual to be delegated to.
- Assess his or her ability.
- Remember that very few jobs can simply be passed over. Many involve some kind of training. Prepare a training plan.

During

- Establish with the person to whom you are delegating the range and implications of the job.
- Train him or her in all aspects.
- Set the limits to his or her authority. While you must give him or her the freedom to make certain decisions as to how the job is carried out, you can set certain limits on that authority.
- Show the person that you trust him or her.
- Agree the timescales.
- Advise anyone who may be affected that you have delegated the task.
- Monitor and support while the person is carrying out the task.
- Appraise progress regularly.
- Praise where praise is due.

After

- Evaluate the success of the delegation.
- Identify any further training needed.

■ Give feedback.

■ Hand over the job permanently.

Monitoring for success

Any person when tackling a task for the first time will make mistakes, not because the task is necessarily difficult, but because it is new.

Mistakes are healthy and important, because it is usually through mistakes that we learn how to improve or change things.

A simple model describes what happens while a person is learning a new task.

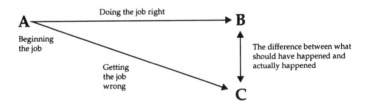

A is the point at which the person begins the job. If all goes well and there are no mistakes then he or she reaches point **B** fairly quickly.

If, however, he or she makes mistakes early on and is not being monitored, then he or she is likely to end up at point **C** which is where the job has been done wrong. At this point, not only do you have to correct the mistake, or even re-do the whole job, but you also have to tell the individual that he or she has failed. If you ever have to do this you are going to demotivate that person, who is unlikely to accept delegated tasks again. It is similar to an aeroplane taking off from London and heading towards Sydney. If the pilot doesn't constantly correct navigation, then going wrong by as little as half a degree can mean the flight can end up at a completely different destination.

Most people when learning a job for the first time, learn something like this:

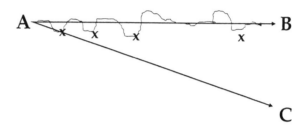

The point marked **X** is where you monitor and put the individual back on course. If you are regularly monitoring, then even though the person may make lots of mistakes, eventually he or she will reach point **B** and will have succeeded. It is *your* responsibility to make sure that he or she succeeds.

How to manage mistakes

You must have experienced times when you have produced a report and given it to your manager to look over, and the first thing he/she spots is a spelling mistake. And then the grammatical errors! And probably not a word is said about how good the report is.

When delegating a task, it is of course your job to keep an eye out for mistakes. However, before pointing the mistakes out, look for the things that have been done right and point those out first. This is called the positive sandwich. Going straight for the jugular is very demotivating for people and their feelings about what you might have to say that is good later will be coloured by how they felt about the mistake you pointed out.

We are often very tempted to fix mistakes for people. Except in dire emergencies you must **always** allow the individual to sort out his or her own mistakes. This helps to build confidence, stops the person relying on you, and helps him or her to learn.

Checklist

- Delegate authority with responsibility.
- Take time to train people properly.
- Point out what's right before pointing out a mistake.
- Praise success.
- Hand over the job.

8

Managing Meetings

Jilly Cooper once remarked that meetings are like cocktail parties. No one wants to go but we get really offended if we are not invited. Meetings, both informal and formal, are the most common way of communicating in the workplace.

Meetings can occur in corridors, by the photocopying machine or more formally in a designated meeting room. The principles discussed in this chapter apply to most kinds of meetings.

Before the meeting

Is the meeting necessary and what is its purpose?

Before calling a meeting you need to ask yourself the question:

"What is the *purpose* of this meeting? Do I need to hold

a meeting or could my purpose be achieved through a telephone call or a memo?"

Sometimes meetings are held that are unnecessary, waste time and irritate people. How often have you come out of a lengthy meeting wondering what the meeting was for and why you were there?

Who should attend the meeting?

The only people who need to attend the meeting are those who either have an item on the agenda, whose views are specifically needed in order to make a decision, or who are going to have to carry out any action.

Do not invite people to attend for the sake of it, or because they need to know what's going on. You can always circulate the minutes to interested parties as well as the participants at the meeting.

Do not ask people to attend the whole meeting if they are only required for one or two items on the agenda. Arrange the agenda so that they can attend the meeting for the sections that are relevant to them and then leave.

The Agenda

The agenda should not be used as the Chair's crib card. It has a specific purpose and that is to inform people of what the purpose of the meeting is, who will be attending, where it is, what time it is, how long it is likely to last, what will be discussed and what preparation they are likely to have to do in order to contribute effectively.

The agenda should list specifically the items to be discussed and the expected outcome, how long they will take and who will be leading that discussion. This way people will be able to anticipate and prepare more effectively for the meeting.

Example agenda

Agenda
House Style Project Meeting

Date:	25 September 1994
Time:	1000
Venue:	Conference Room 2, Quadrant Court
Attendees:	Sam Peters, Tony Carter, Peter Field, Annie Fell, Nancy Park, Gary Toms

Time	Subject	
1015	Apologies for absence	
	Update on actions from previous meeting	
1030	**Installation of new typeface**	Gary Toms
	Update and report on progress	
1050	**House style manual**	Annie Fell
	Review and agreement of sections 1–3	
1110	**Implementation date**	Sam Peters
	Discussion and agreement on feasible implementation date	
1120	**Handouts**	Sam Peters
	Consultation and discussion on method of production	
1150	**Binding of reports**	Tony Carter
	Report back and recommendations on what we should buy	
1205	**Training**	Peter Field
	Recommendations and timetable	
1220	**Summary and Action points**	
1235	End of meeting	

Any papers that need to be discussed at the meeting should be sent out with the agenda to the participants so that they have a chance to read them in advance. This means that you don't waste time during the meeting waiting for people to read papers that they could have read at another time.

Send out the agenda in enough time so that people have time to read any relevant papers and prepare for the meeting.

Never put AOB (any other business) on the agenda. It encourages people not to let you know in advance what they want to discuss. This means that you cannot prepare, and have no idea how long the item is going to take.

Make it clear to people that you will not accept AOB and that you must have agenda items in advance.

If this really isn't possible, then make AOB the first item on the agenda. Before you tackle any of the other items, ask what the AOB is and decide there and then whether you will slot it into the meeting and where you will put it. Or, you may decide that it isn't relevant to this meeting.

The venue and timing

Make sure that the meeting is as conveniently situated for people as possible. Even for small team meetings, always try and find a private room away from telephones and distractions.

Never hold a meeting on a Monday morning or a Friday afternoon. People are not at their best then. On Monday mornings they're thinking about what's coming up that week and they really need the time to plan. Friday afternoons people want to finish things off and are thinking about getting home.

To get people to the meeting on time, don't hold meetings on the hour or half hour. Hold them at quarter past and quarter to the hour. People have a psychology which means they are more likely to be on time for 'odd' hours than they are for normal ones.

The minute taker

If you are holding a departmental or team meeting, don't assume that the secretary should automatically take the minutes, they are also part of the team. It is very difficult for someone to be fully involved in the meeting if he or she is trying to take minutes at the same time. For team meetings you should rotate the minute taker amongst members of your team.

Always agree with the minute taker the purpose and objectives of each item on the agenda. Encourage the minute taker to ask questions for clarification and summarise after every agenda item so that you can all agree on what the actions are during the meeting.

During the meeting

Always make sure you start the meeting on time. If you wait for people to arrive everyone will know that you will wait so they won't bother trying to get to the next meeting on time either. Also, the people who did turn up on time will get annoyed and won't bother being punctual in the future.

When latecomers do arrive, acknowledge their apologies, but do not stop the meeting and don't bring them up to date with what they have missed. Again, this encourages people not to be late.

When you have welcomed everyone, make sure that they have all received an agenda and check for anyone who may need to leave early. Clarify the objectives of the agenda and each item and remind people of the timings against each item.

Stick to the agenda and the timings against it. It is important that you finish meetings on time and that means that you mustn't over run time on individual agenda items.

Keep control of the meeting by constantly asking the minute taker to summarise and by summarising yourself, and make sure that everyone knows and has written down his or her action points and deadlines.

At the end of the meeting summarise all the action points again.

To close the meeting, end on a positive note. Thank people for their contribution and give brief details of the next meeting if appropriate.

After the meeting

As the Chair of the meeting you are responsible for ensuring that action is taken. It is not enough just to leave it to the participants. Besides which, there is nothing more frustrating than asking for action results at a meeting only to discover that the person who was supposed to action it hasn't done so.

Keep a note of individuals' agreed actions in either the bring forward system or your rolling to do list. Chase people up in advance of the agreed deadline for results.

Send out the minutes of the meeting as quickly as possible. The minutes act as a further reminder to people that they had agreed to take some action.

Unless there is a legal requirement to do so, the minutes only need to contain a note of the agreed action. They do not need to be verbatim minutes because what matters is not so much what people *said* at the meeting, but what they agreed to *do*. Don't waste time producing verbatim minutes. They are not needed and people won't read them anyway.

When sending out the minutes to the participants, highlight the actions that they agreed to.

Example

House Style Project Meeting

Action notes from meeting held on 25 September 1994

Present: Sam Peters, Tony Carter, Peter Field, Annie Fell, Nancy Park, Gary Toms

Apologies: **None**

cc: **Simon Baker**

	Action	By
Installation of new typeface		
This is on schedule. Major problems with technology in use at people's homes. Gary to progress.	GT	31 July
House style manual		
Content agreed. Section 1 needs revision. Annie Fell to circulate new version.	AF	27 July
Implementation date		
Confirmed as 1 September 1994. Date to be briefed to all staff in August.	All	31 August
Handouts		
Method of punctuation to be as outlined in Sam's paper (attached).	SP	17 July
Binding of reports		
Binders to be ordered immediately.	TC	21 July
Training		
Training will start in September and run through until Christmas.	PF	1 August
Next meeting		

The next meeting will be held on Thursday 18 August at 1015 in room 417.

Checklist

- Make sure that a meeting is the best way of achieving your objective.
- Only ask people to attend if they really need to be there.
- Do an agenda that is specific and timed.
- Start the meeting on time.
- Summarise after each agenda item.
- Agree actions during the meeting.
- Keep minutes of the actions.
- It's your responsibility as the Chair to chase actions.

Working with a Secretary

Most managers do not use their secretaries in the best possible way to help them to manage their time and workload better. At worst they use them to answer or make telephone calls, organise tea and coffee, and fetch visitors.

There is also a misconception that the time of the person who is paid the most is more important than the time of the person who is paid less. This is an understandable attitude in view of the way organisations often charge out for people's time.

However, in reality, pay bears little or no relation to the importance of a person's time. The importance of a person's time is based upon what task he or she is performing at a particular time and what the consequences are of the task not getting done. For example, if your secretary is typing a report that you have to present to an important client tomorrow, then for that period, his or her time is more important than yours.

This is one of the biggest errors managers make. They barely leave themselves enough time to get their own jobs done properly and then they wonder why the secretary can't produce the work to the deadline. We constantly hear stories of secretaries who have to stay late to type reports and so on that their managers have left to the last minute. Your time as a manager is not yours alone.

Everything that you do or don't do affects how well your secretary manages his or her time. At best, it makes for lots of fire-fighting. At worst, it is inconsiderate and results in poorly produced work and a demotivated secretary.

Managing the diary

Your secretary should have absolute control of your diary. You should always route requests for appointments through to the secretary.

- Put aside time every day to speak to your secretary about your workload.
- Never make your own appointments. Let your secretary arrange whatever appointments you need.
- The secretary should keep the master copy of the diary. You should only have a slave copy with you for reference.
- Make sure that the secretary has in the diary your task appointments as well as other kinds so that s/he doesn't book a meeting over a time you have set aside for a really important task.

- Sit down with your secretary and go through the diary on a daily basis. If you are out of the office, then you should ring in at least twice a day for any diary changes and messages.
- Set aside in your diary two periods each week of at least two hours to do general paperwork.
- Remember that when you commit yourself to something in your diary, particularly if it's an appointment to do a job, failure to do it results in your secretary looking bad and feeling frustrated.

Setting and managing deadlines

Every deadline you agree has a knock on effect on your secretary. You must remember that you are not one person in your job, you are two people and you need to take into account the needs and problems of your secretary when agreeing to deadlines.

- When you are discussing your workload with your secretary, find out what his or her workload is, too.
- Set realistic deadlines for your secretary to produce work. For instance, does all typing really have to go out within twenty-four hours? You may think that it takes only ten minutes to type a letter, but you need to bear in mind that the secretary will have to reference, file, find out the correct address, correct, amend, print copies, type an envelope, photocopy and produce the enclosures (always supposing they are immediately to hand).
- On every piece of work that you give your secretary, put a "by when" date.

Dealing with interruptions

Your secretary is a very useful tool to help you to manage interruptions. A common mistake most managers make is that they believe they should be available to their teams, their bosses and their customers at all times. This is not the case. You are frequently unavailable to all these people, simply because you are in a meeting or on holiday or visiting a customer.

Managers often think that the only person who suffers because of being interrupted is themselves. In fact, every time you allow yourself to be interrupted you are effectively interrupting your secretary. By allowing yourself to be interrupted you are disrupting your work flow. This means that you will begin to get behind with things and ultimately this will affect your secretary's ability to do the job.

- Ask your secretary to filter your phone calls.
- Make it a two way relationship. If your secretary is busy doing something really important for you, then offer to answer the telephone for a while.
- If you need to speak to people on the telephone, get your secretary to make a telephone appointment just as they would make an appointment for you to have a meeting.
- Don't ask your secretary to get people on the phone for you. That wastes the secretary's time and often when he or she has the person on the line, you will be on the telephone to someone else. Make your own phone calls as often as you reasonably can.
- Delegate some phone calls to your secretary that you don't need to personally handle.
- Set aside time in your diary when you are available to see or speak to anyone without an appointment.

- Allow your secretary to make the decisions about who can and can't interrupt you.
- Often the secretary will be by-passed by visitors who will be asking you to do things that really the secretary could do. If this happens, pass the visitor back to the secretary.
- If a telephone caller insists on speaking to you and you know it's something that your secretary could deal with, pass the call back.

Managing post and paperwork

- Make sure your secretary understands the work that you do.
- Don't open your own post and don't give into the temptation to flick through it while it's on the secretary's desk.
- Encourage your secretary to read all your mail.
- Agree with your secretary a time each day (with alternatives for when you are out of the office) when you will go through the post. *You do not need to have your secretary with you while you are looking at your post.*
- Give your secretary the power and authority to pass on mail addressed to you that can be more appropriately be dealt with by someone else.
- Allow your secretary to draft replies for you that you can simply agree and sign.
- Encourage your secretary to write letters in his or her own name.

Passing work to and receiving work from the secretary

- Do not interrupt the secretary. Remember that his or her time is often as important as yours. Particularly don't interrupt your secretary to fetch you coffee. He or she is a secretary – not a servant!

■ As you are going through the day write a list of the things that you would like the secretary to do and give it to him or her at regular intervals. All the secretary then needs to do is to make a note by the side of each instruction to let you know what has happened and pass the piece of paper back to you. You can then throw it away.

■ If you prefer to handwrite your letters, make sure that you attach to your handwritten document a copy of the letter that you are replying to.

■ Always put deadlines against any notes for the secretary's action.

■ Make sure that you set aside regular times during the day/week when you sit down with the secretary and go through whatever needs to be discussed face to face.

Delegating to the secretary

Be sensible and delegate as much as you can to your secretary. Some jobs are exclusively the secretary's. You are not delegating if you simply allow him or her to do the job he or she is paid to do. For example:

■ managing the diary
■ opening and sorting the mail
■ filing
■ fact-finding
■ arranging travel
■ arranging meetings
■ first line for answering the telephone

When thinking about delegating to your secretary, think laterally. Don't make assumptions about intelligence levels or ability or even credibility. Assume your secretary could do most of your job and start from there.

Some examples of things you might delegate are:

- research
- doing the monthly accounts
- reading (and summarising for you) trade magazines, reports etc.
- attending internal meetings on your behalf
- writing regular reports
- replying to correspondence
- internal project work

Checklist

- Make sure your secretary fully understands the objectives and priorities of your job.
- Regularly discuss with your secretary both your workload and his/hers.
- Set realistic deadlines.
- Use your secretary to deal with interruptions.
- Give your secretary responsibility and authority to deal with the post on your behalf.
- Don't interrupt your secretary.
- Delegate.

Managing Stress

A major influence on how effectively we deal with and manage our time and workload is the amount of stress we are under. Being over or under-stressed has a big impact on our ability to be effective and in control at work.

In *The Mind Survey: Stress at Work* a fifth of companies attributed up to 50% of all days off sick to stress related illness and some people have estimated that 100 million working days in the UK are lost due to stress. This has a massive impact on the ability of an organisation to be productive. This results in more pressure being put on the individuals who aren't off sick, sometimes resulting in their feeling stressed, and needing time off work and so on. Stress, unless dealt with, can be a vicious circle of poor productivity and low morale.

It is something that needs to be taken seriously, although not over-reacted to, because as this chapter shows, stress is a very individual thing and only individuals can really tackle the problems. However organisations can put in place systems and mechanisms to help their employees to cope.

What is stress?

Stress is essentially a term used to describe the pressure that is being put on us, coming either internally or externally. Stress in itself is not necessarily a bad thing. It has come to mean something negative, but in fact is actually necessary to sustain our lives.

Essentially, stress is caused when either supports or constraints are out of balance, making us question our ability to meet the demand.

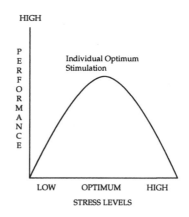

When we are at our optimum stress levels our performance is enhanced. We are positive, creative, calm, in control and effective. If we are either under or over-stressed then our performance, behaviour and mood suffers as a consequence.

Stress is different for different people and what causes one individual to feel stressed may not cause another individual to feel the same way.

Symptoms of stress

Stress shows itself differently for different people. It normally manifests itself under three kinds of symptoms: physical, emotional and behavioural.

Physical

Physical symptoms include:

- headaches
- poor skin
- stomach upsets
- high blood pressure
- lank hair
- lots of illnesses such as colds and flu
- hyperventilating
- heart trouble
- insomnia
- over-tiredness

Emotional

Emotional symptoms include:

- bad or short tempered
- tearful
- feelings of anxiety/worry
- paranoia
- anger and frustration
- feeling of powerlessness and loss of control

Behavioural

Behavioural symptoms include:

- snapping at people
- being generally lethargic
- being hyper-active
- inability to concentrate
- generally disorganised
- constantly misplacing things

These are just examples of some of the symptoms relating to stress. It is different for different people. The key is to recognise what your symptoms of stress are so that as soon as they appear you can begin to take action to deal with your stress.

It is worth noting here that the symptoms of over-stress and under-stress can often be very similar. If things are too easy for us – that is, we have lots of supports and not enough constraints (i.e. the job we do is too easy for us and doesn't challenge us) then we are likely to experience some of the same sorts of symptoms that we get if we are over-stressed. Either way, it is important to recognise them for ourselves.

Animals in zoos experience under-stress since they do not have to hunt for their food or work for their survival because they are fed and sheltered by the zoo staff. This can cause lethargy or aggression in these animals because there are too many supports and not enough constraints.

Identifying Likely Stressors

Having recognised your symptoms of stress you then need to identify those things which actually cause you personal stress, either over or under your own optimum level.

For example, it may be that you are a real stickler for punctuality and you find it stressful to be running late for meetings, or to have other people arrive late. Others may not bother about punctuality at all and will therefore not get stressed by it. One of the key things to note here is that you mustn't assume that what is important to you (and therefore likely to stress you if it goes wrong) is not necessarily important to others. People are stressed by different things. You need to identify your own stress list.

Having done that, you are now in a better position to estimate at what periods during your life you are likely to feel stressed and take action to deal with it in advance where possible.

If you are feeling over-stressed it can become a vicious circle. You feel stressed so your performance drops, which means you make more mistakes and you take longer to do things, all of which adds to the stress.

Ask yourself the following questions:

- On the whole, am I happy in my job?
- Do I have the right tools (materials/equipment) to carry out my job satisfactorily?
- Do I have a good working relationship with my manager, team and colleagues and do I feel supported by them?
- Is my working environment right for what I need to do?

- Am I spending too much time either at work, working at home or worrying about work?
- Do I have enough leisure time?
- Do I have enough time to spend on myself?
- Am I coping financially?
- Do I have a good network of friends and family to support me?
- Do I spend too much time travelling?
- Is my home environment comfortable and to my taste?
- Do I have enough to do at work? Too little? Too much?

Read each of the statements below and tick any that apply to you when you are under pressure

1. I am easily irritated ☐

2. I have difficulty concentrating for any length of time ☐

3. I feel tired even when I wake up in the morning ☐

4. I have difficulty making even simple decisions ☐

5. The quality of my sleep has deteriorated. I have difficulty getting to sleep and/or I wake during the night and am restless ☐

6. I lose my temper frequently ☐

7. I feel powerful negative emotions ☐

8. I feel generally run down and unwell ☐

9. Life seems to be quite hopeless. Nothing seems worthwhile and I feel really low ☐

10. My eating pattern has altered. I have lost my appetite or I seem to be eating more food to comfort myself   □

11. I have difficulty in absorbing new data   □

12. I suffer from frequent headaches   □

13. I have difficulty recalling information when I am required to do so   □

14. I am drinking more alcohol than usual   □

15. I experience dramatic swings of mood   □

16. I have missed, or been late, for one or two important appointments   □

17. I feel wound up and unable to relax properly   □

18. I am unable to achieve my normal level of creativity   □

19. I suffer from backache regularly   □

20. I feel inadequate and unable to cope   □

21. I have taken time off work   □

22. I suffer from indigestion   □

23. I seem to lack the capacity to focus on a particular problem. My mind keeps wandering on to other issues   □

24. The least little thing sends me into a panic   □

25. I smoke more cigarettes than usual   □

26. I have a frequent need to urinate   □

27. In discussion with other people I frequently
    repeat myself   □

28. My driving is rather erratic and my
    judgement is impaired   □

29. I seem to spend all my time worrying   □

30. I feel very lethargic and uninterested in work
    and/or life   □

Looking at the number of ticks on this list will help you to identify when you are under stress so that you can take steps to deal with it.

Perceptions and causes of stress

Essentially there are five main causes of stress:

- Our perception of the demand placed upon us
- The fact that our constraints and supports are not balanced
- One bit of our life jigsaw is either too big or missing
- If we are asked to do something which challenges our sense of self (i.e., ethics and values)
- If we are experiencing a period of major change (either positive, welcome change or negative, unwelcome change)

Perceptions

The world does not exist in fact, it exists only in our perception of it. For example, we believe it to be a fact that grass is green. This is because we see the grass as green. However, many animals do not have colour vision and do not see grass as green but as a sort of brownish greyish colour, so for them grass is not green. Similarly, there are some people who we really dislike, yet there are other people who like them very much. There are some jobs that we do well, and others we can't do at all, there are some subjects that we were very good at or bad at at school, and yet others felt differently about them.

It is important to recognise that the world is only as *we see it*, because that helps us to realise that often feeling over-stressed is not a fact but a perception based on how we feel about the situation that we are in.

Recognising that the world also only exists through our perceptions of it helps us to recognise that in order to reduce our stress level we can simply change our perception of the situation that we are in.

One common aspect of human behaviour is called awfulising. Awfulising means imagining the worst about a situation before it has even happened. The worst rarely does happen.

We need to learn to be more realistic when anticipating problems. Ask yourself what's the worst thing that can happen and work from there. It's also about using your common sense – for instance, if you're not normally late for work, you're very unlikely to be sacked because you overslept! Don't awfulise. Look at the situation for what it really is. Very few things are a matter of life and death, particularly at work.

Your life jigsaw

People's lives are a bit like jigsaws. Every bit has a different function and we feel differently about it. The trick is to keep all the pieces in proportion and in the right size. That way, if one bit of the jigsaw is out of balance, all the other bits will help to give us a sense of proportion.

Five ways of dealing with stress

There are essentially five ways of dealing with stress.

- Understanding and acceptance of self
- Tackling the problem
- Self-nurturing
- Emotional expression
- Active distraction

Understanding and acceptance of self

In order to be able to cope with stress you need to:

- understand your needs and motives
- know your own values and priorities
- accept yourself and your limitations
- recognise your stressors

You need to be honest with yourself and where your demands come from. The reality is you will often place higher demands on yourself than others ever do. Often the demands you set yourself are irrational and impossible to achieve – being the perfect manager, never making mistakes, being the perfect partner, producing the perfect document etc.

Trying to be perfect leads to burnout. When we are under stress, we often make it worse by trying to be all things to all people and become so busy being busy that we don't leave time to look after ourselves and end up not looking after anyone.

Identify and clarify, both to yourself and others, your values and priorities. If you don't communicate them to people, they won't understand what the problem is. It is perfectly legitimate to believe that attending your child's sports day is more important than a meeting at work, even if it is with the Managing Director. However, not everyone feels like that, so you mustn't assume that they will. They are more likely to understand what your priorities and values are if you explain them.

Similarly, you may need to go into work one weekend (although of course you should avoid spending too much of your home time working as this contributes massively to stress levels). This may be perfectly legitimate. By explaining to your family why you need to go in and the importance of it they are more likely to understand.

Understand yourself. When experiencing stress, don't automatically look around to find someone to blame it on. Look first inside yourself and find out what's going on there. Are you awfulising, or blaming the cause of stress on something other than the real problem? Are you taking out your work frustrations at home or vice versa?

Dealing with stress means understanding yourself. It means dealing not just with the world around you, but with the world within you.

> *Not in the clamour of the crowded street*
> *Not in the shouts and plaudits of the throng*
> *But in ourselves, are triumph and defeat.*
> *Henry Longfellow*

Tackling the problem

When you are feeling over-stressed, the first thing to do is to see if you can remove the cause of the stress. You need, however, to remember that the symptom is not always the same as the problem. For example, if you are feeling over-loaded at work, the problem may not be that you are over-loaded, but that you haven't been trained in a particular aspect of your job properly. You must tackle the **problem,** not the symptom, because if you only deal with the symptom then the real problem will never go away and will appear again later on.

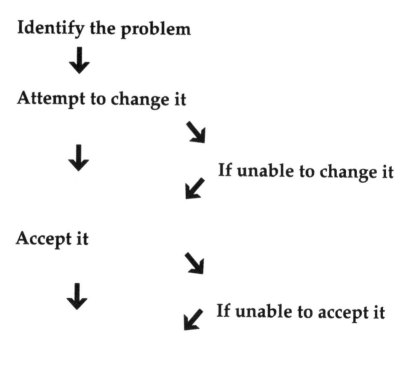

Identify the problem

⬇

Attempt to change it

⬇　　　↘

　　　　If unable to change it　↙

Accept it

⬇　　　↘

　　　　If unable to accept it　↙

Move away

If you can sort the problem out then you should do so. If you really can't sort it out then you need to accept it and move on.

It is pointless worrying or getting upset about things that you can do absolutely nothing about.

Self-nurturing

When you are suffering from an excess of stress, it is particularly important that you look after yourself. This means taking the time to feed and care for both your body and your mind. Usually, however, when stressed, we tend to forget our own needs, lose our sense of self-esteem and generally add to our feeling of worthlessness.

Think of your body as if it were a car. Stress is like the choke – a little choke is good for you and gives your body the kick-start it needs to operate. However, if you leave the choke out all day it damages the engine and raises the fuel consumption. If you notice something wrong with your car – smoke coming out of the engine or backfiring – you don't drive it faster. You are more likely to slow down, and maybe even take it into a garage for a check up.

If you push yourself too hard you are likely to overheat your mental, emotional and body engines. The first step is to boost your self image and then look after your body.

Boosting self image

- Buy yourself a present
- Lock yourself away in the bathroom with a warm bath and a good book

- Do something you like doing
- Accept compliments and give them
- Find some time to completely relax
- Praise yourself when you do well
- Fish for compliments!

Looking after yourself

- Eat healthily with a balanced diet (this doesn't mean denying yourself food you like but making sure you eat plenty of the stuff that's good for you too!)
- Get some exercise (walking, swimming, playing a sport you enjoy)
- Try to get a good night's sleep

Emotional expression

When we are under a lot of stress, one of the most common human reactions is to refuse help, become withdrawn and begin to feel isolated. This is the time when we most need support networks around us – family and friends.

We also try to hide how we are feeling, thinking that we shouldn't bring our feelings into work, or that people won't want to listen, or that if we show how we are feeling others might think that we are incompetent.

Of course, as long as we keep those feelings blocked inside then no one *can* help us and we probably can't help ourselves.

To be healthy and energetic we need to maintain positive emotions and not let the negative ones take over. In order to do this we need to express our feelings in a way that is appropriate in terms of timing and the audience.

Take action by:

- developing a support network, both at work and at home, of people who you can share your feelings honestly with and who will give you common sense views
- have regular two-way communication with your manager, your colleagues and your team
- tell people how you feel about a particular thing. You don't have to burst into tears or rush out of the room in a temper, but you can say "I feel very angry about that." This is a way of getting your feelings known without actually shouting at people
- Accept that emotions are actually OK and that everyone has them
- Share your feelings with someone you trust

Active distraction

Active distraction means doing something that forces us not to think about whatever it is that is causing us to feel stressed. When we feel particularly under pressure we have a tendency to dwell on whatever it is that is causing us the problem even at times when there is nothing we can do about it. How many times have we woken up at 2am, worrying about a problem at work yet things frequently feel less bad and less important the next day.

When we get home from work there is nothing we can do about the work problem, and when we are at work there is usually nothing we can do about the home problem. Put things where they belong and do something that forces you to think about something else.

Examples might include:

- read a good, absorbing book
- take some exercise (particularly a team game where you have to concentrate on the game)
- go out to the cinema or the theatre
- socialise with your friends
- do your hobby

Checklist: How to avoid unhealthy stress

- Ask – what's the worst that can happen?
- Put things into perspective
- Aim for a good home/work balance
- Don't be a perfectionist
- Recognise that guilt is a useless emotion
- Move on from the past
- Focus on today
- Identify five good things that you have, or have happened, each day
- Leave work at work and home at home
- Have a healthy lifestyle – exercise, eat a balanced diet, leave time in your week to spend on yourself

Balancing Work and Home

Home life and work life are equally important and we want to make the most of both. The problem comes when we cannot balance them and we are faced with either internal or external conflict.

Clearly, things will not be in balance all the time. There are occasions when we are involved in a particularly important project at work, which entails working quite a bit in our spare time. There is actually nothing wrong with this, provided that we then redress the balance at home at some point. Similarly a situation at home may require a lot of time and attention, and we might find that we are not concentrating at work as much as we would like. Again, this is not a problem provided that at some point we are able to turn our attention to our priorities there too.

The problem arises most often however when work begins to creep far too much into our home life. Many people put work first, probably because they feel that they are paid to work and they need the money, therefore it deserves their undivided attention. Well, certainly it deserves attention, but so do our families and ourselves.

Focusing too much on either work or home (normally work) causes us to feel guilty and pressured, and this results in considerable stress. The stress can then make us lose all sense of priorities and not concentrate enough on **any** of the aspects of our lives.

The choices are the same for both men and women. However, many women perceive the conflicts in balancing work and home to be more acute, as they often feel that they are the prime carers and homemakers.

Balancing work and home is essentially about deciding on priorities both long term and at any given moment, and making choices about where we choose to spend our time.

Establishing the priorities

- The starting point is to establish how much of your precious time over the next month you are prepared to give to each of the demands you have placed upon you. You need to think ahead, because we are so unconscious of time slipping by that sometimes we discover that in a month, we have spent most of our evenings and weekends working and have not given as much time to our family, friends and ourselves as we would really like to.

Once you begin to add up the amount of time you have available, you can begin to make sensible choices about those things on which you *really* want to spend your time.

It is important to note here that you shouldn't go overboard accounting for every moment of your time. Otherwise, you'll create stress for yourself. However, it helps to have an idea of how little available time there is, so that if you do nothing with that time, it's because you have made a positive choice and not because time is slipping by without your being aware of it.

There are three stages to balancing all these different demands, needs and priorities:

1. Working out what is important to you
2. Being able to communicate this to others
3. Being able to negotiate with others to protect what is important to you

1 Working out what is important to you

- identify clearly the things that you value in your life
- give them a rating e.g., children 10, partner 10, work 8, hobbies 7, reading 8, spending time alone 9, watching TV 5

2 Being able to communicate this to others

- evaluate how much of your time at present you are spending on the things you value and how much of it is being frittered away on things that you don't want to spend your time doing
- remember that you cannot make *more* time, you can only choose to spend it more wisely
- tell people what's important to you

- don't agree to do things that you don't want to do unless there is a really good reason for it
- ask people for the things that you need to help you to achieve your priorities
- learn how to say no

Chores

- play the 'I have to, or else . . .' game
- make a list of all the things that you have to do at home or at work that are 'chores'
- having made the list, ask someone to challenge what you have written
- make sure that for each thing on the list you are asking the question 'Why do *I* have to do this? What are the consequences of its not being done? What will I gain by not doing it?'

The list can be endless, and certainly worth challenging. You have to ask yourself the question 'What is more important RIGHT NOW? Is it doing the dishes or is it sitting down and spending some time talking with my partner/children?' Allow yourself the freedom to choose not to do those things if they are clashing with the things that actually **really** matter to you.

Examine your own attitudes towards these things. Think about raising your dirt tolerance level, or your desire to produce gourmet meals for your family every night. Give yourself permission to have soup and bread one night, or cook a stew that lasts all week etc.

Being able to negotiate with others

Use other people to help you. Having a wide range of contacts, both family and friends, is not just about emotional support, but also about practical help. Why not think about employing extra help at home (e.g., for the housework or the garden), if you can afford it. Paying someone else to do this is the clear choice between money and time. Which is more valuable to you? Would you rather keep the money and spend less time with your family?

Also, use your family. If you are a woman, are you always the one who washes, cooks, cleans, irons, nags, gets everyone up in the morning (so often the self-determined woman's role). Are the rest of your family pulling their weight? Don't just share out jobs, share out accountability for those jobs too. Worrying about whether or not there's food in the fridge is often worse than having to cook it! Bear in mind, though, that if you delegate accountability for tasks to others in your family, you have to accept that they may not be done to your standards.

Above all, make sure that you allow time for leisure activities – the 'me' time. If you are tired and over-stressed because you are not allowing time for yourself to recuperate and recharge your batteries, you will not be giving either work or home your best.

Keep as much of a balance as you can between time spent working and time spent being at home.

Most of us are prepared to accept that in reality there will be peaks and troughs in our working lives when we will have to pull out all the stops. The difficulty comes when this way of working becomes expected and habitual.

If you find you are in the habit of spending more time at work than you would like, ask yourself the following questions:

- how much do I actually produce during those extra hours?
- are there more flexible ways in which I could work and still be productive?

Use the hours at work to produce, break the pattern of staying late regularly. Wherever possible, use normal working hours for telephone calls, meetings, seminars and courses. However tempting, avoid setting up anything before breakfast, after work or at weekends.

Remember that you need to make a **life** as well as a living and that your family and friends have as much right to some of your time as your employer does.

Checklist

- Aim for a balance
- Put work at work and home at home
- Be conscious of how much time you are spending on your priorities and how much on things that really aren't that important
- Tell others what's important to you
- Delegate chores
- Make time for yourself

Bibliography

Do Yourself A Favour
Allcock, Debra (The Industrial Society 1993)
Delegation
Forrest, Andrew (The Industrial Society 1989)
Making Meetings Work
Barker, Alan (The Industrial Society 1993)
Working With A Secretary
Allcock, Debra (The Industrial Society 1993)
The Administration Game Workbook (The Industrial Society 1995)
The Stress Workbook
Warren, Eve and Tell, Caroline (Nicholas Brealey Publishing 1992)